Different Roads

By Kathy Troccoli

J COUNTRYMAN®

Acknowledgments

I would like to thank . . .

All the women who contributed to this book. You have ministered His life to me.
Linda, my faithful assistant, for doing and giving way beyond what I ask for.
Erickson & Baugher for continuing on a journey with me where dreams become reality.
Jack Countryman and staff for this wonderful opportunity to encourage
the hearts of thousands.

Copyright © 1999 by Kathy Troccoli

Published by J. Countryman, a division of Thomas Nelson, Inc., Nashville, Tennessee 37214.

Project editor—Terri Gibbs

All rights reserved. No portion of this publication may be reproduced, stored in a retrieval system or transmitted in any form by any means—electronic, mechanical, photocopying, recording, or any other—except for brief quotations in printed reviews, without the prior written permission of the publisher.

Unless other wise indicated, all Scripture quotations in this book are from the New International Version of the Bible (NIV), copyright © 1973, 1978, 1984 by the International Bible Society and are used by permission of Zondervan Publishing House.

J. Countryman is a trademark of Thomas Nelson Inc.

Designed by Koechel Peterson & Associates, Inc.
Minneapolis, Minnesota.

ISBN: 08499-5502-5

Printed and bound in the United States of America

Foreword

What a joy it has been to create a book for women written by women. As I travel and sing I meet thousands upon thousands of precious women—each with a unique story, each having traveled a different road. I've had tender conversations, I've had my shirts stained with tears, I've smiled and rejoiced until my face hurt, and I've wrapped my arms around a broken heart.

I have asked several women to contribute to this book and have included some of my favorite quotes and Scriptures. Recently I learned that a dear friend was diagnosed with breast cancer and would have to have a double mastectomy. I sobbed . . . lost sleep . . . and wrestled with God. That same day I received the first entries for this book, and as I read them, I was gently reminded how real and faithful God is. For what I had hoped this book would give to you, He was already giving back to me!

I am constantly in awe of what God can and will do in our lives. I have seen Him work time and time again through the lives of ordinary yet remarkable women, like those in this book. I pray that through their stories you will be encouraged, ignited, surrendered, and broken—to believe Him, serve Him, and love Him as He leads you down your own special road.

Kathy Troccoli
March 1999

It is the Lord who goes before you,

He will not fail you or forsake you.

Deuteronomy 31:8

Free-Wheeling Down a Reckless Road

When I was six years old, I got the bright idea I'd teach myself how to ride a bike. But rather than use one of the small bikes scattered around our hill-top yard, I was determined to make a grand debut on my older brother's bike. It was twice my size.

I rolled the monstrous bike over to Grandmother's flowerbed, stood on the red brick ledge around it, and climbed over the awful bar that makes a bike a boy's. After tipping over into the petunias half a dozen times, I finally shoved off successfully and began to peddle and balance. Before I had a mere moment to throw back my head and feel the wind in my face, however, I realized I was heading straight for the road that curved down the hill to the highway. I had learned how to peddle, but I had not learned how to stop.

I began free-wheeling down the hill, my knees knocking so badly the bike went into a full wobble. I was a sight to behold. My mouth was wide open, but I couldn't utter a sound. The tooth fairy had gone bankrupt on my four front teeth so my tonsils were fully exposed. The fancy rubber bands with the green see-through balls holding up my pigtails had sprung and gone. My brown eyes were bulging. My feet had left the pedals, and my bony legs were sticking straight out in the wind. It wasn't pretty.

There was no time to think. I simply dropped down to the bar and dragged both bare feet on the gravel-covered asphalt. Thankfully, pain gave way to poor steering, and I ended up in a ditch of Arkansas pine needles. True to form, I covered my eyes until I could muster the courage to look through my fingers at my poor, pitiful feet. The sight shocked the sound back into my vocal cords, and—so they tell me—I could be heard all over the Ouachita Hills.

> I have chosen the way of truth. I run in the path of your commands, for you have set my heart free.
>
> PSALM 119:30, 32

Unfortunately, that wasn't my last reckless ride . . . or my last painful crash. By the time I hopped on my brother's bike for the first time, I was already the victim of something far more dangerous: a secret abuser posing as someone I should trust. Some of my childhood experiences were so traumatic my subconscious tucked them far away in a secret chest. As a teenager I had no idea what kept steering me to fear, insecurity, and self-destruction. I only knew I kept heading down that same reckless road . . . and could never figure out how to use the brakes.

A saint is not one who never falls; it is one who gets up and goes on every time he falls.

ANONYMOUS

I was raised in church but had never been taught how to overcome life-strangling strongholds through the Word of God or to know the Savior who came to set the captives free. In fact, I never realized I *was* a prisoner until Christ began to set me free. When bondage is the only world you've known . . . it's home.

Slowly but surely, the more I studied, believed, and memorized Scripture, the less recklessly I drove myself. I still took the road down the hill sometimes, but eventually I learned how to apply the brakes. I was finally able to recognize my pull toward the wrong road and exposed the damaged places in my heart to the light of God's healing love. The draw down the hill didn't go away for a very long time, but I learned to read the warning signs and pause at the top. And cry. Then, slowly . . . but surely . . . I learned how to take a different road.

Beth Moore

The Sometimes Bumpy Road of Life

Mommy. What a beautiful word. And how I longed to hear it.

My own mother died when I was just fourteen years old. It was a very confusing time in my life. I couldn't understand how God could take her when I needed her so badly. My greatest comfort was the hope that some day I would be a mom with my own precious child.

Nine years after my mother's death I married my kindergarten sweetheart. That's right, my mom and future mother-in-law became friends while we were finger-painting. I love knowing that Mom knew my husband—even if he was only five, pulled my hair, and was shorter than I.

My husband and I had always loved children and looked forward to being parents. We tried to conceive for many years and supplemented our intense prayers and fasting with calisthenics, temperature charts, and doctors. We thought surely there was something we could do besides "wait on the Lord." We were driving down a weary road with bumps, curves, jolting stops, and a big DO NOT ENTER posted at Parenthood Street.

I turned to God's Word, my hope and faith strengthened by His promises. I especially loved to read about Hanna, Rachel, Sarah, and Elizabeth. All of these women ached for a baby, and God blessed them in His time.

After twelve years we, too, were blessed through adoption with a beautiful baby boy. His name means "God's gracious gift." Our lives are complete now, and my face aches from smiling!

It has been twenty years since my mom died. I am amazed how life can change, erasing years of pain in an instant. My heart is full; I wouldn't change a thing. With God nothing is impossible. He never leaves us and has a wonderful plan for our lives. We just have to trust His timing and let Him do the driving down the sometimes bumpy road of life!

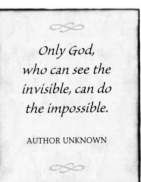

Only God, who can see the invisible, can do the impossible.

AUTHOR UNKNOWN

Barbara

Choosing the Right Path

I had it all figured out.

I was getting ready to graduate from college, and my plan was to get a graduate degree, find a teaching position at a university in Western Canada, buy a house in the mountains, and go snowboarding every weekend. It was going to be quite a life. What a shock when just three months later I was living and working on the East Coast of the United States. Talk about a different road!

My life to that point had been fairly predictable. My parents had lived in the same house all their married life. My father held the same job, and my mother stayed at home with the kids. Life was pretty idyllic. But I was asleep—and taking most of it for granted.

I was very involved in politics and was selected to participate in a weekend training program in Calgary, Alberta, just south of my hometown. That weekend I was selected to participate in a three-month internship with a political think-tank in Washington, D.C., starting in January. My mother still refers to that as the weekend that changed my life forever.

> "I know the plans I have for you," declares the Lord, "plans to prosper you and not to harm you, plans to give hope and a future."
>
> JEREMIAH 29:11

Sure enough, no more than two weeks into the internship I was offered a permanent position. In spite of the many friendships, family, and intricately laid plans waiting for me in Canada, I found myself quickly accepting the position. I had reflected more than once that God has a way of cutting a path through the woods to help us choose the right way. This time I couldn't help but feel that He had paved a highway!

It's been seven years now since I first moved to the United States, and I'm stunned to think of all that has happened. I have no graduate degree, I haven't been snowboarding in years, I work for a ministry, I live in a pitiful little apartment in Arlington, Virginia—but I've never been happier.

In the midst of all my diligent plans and hopes, God had an even better plan for my life—a plan that took me down a most remarkable road.

Carolyn Meraw

The Road I Never Planned to Take

Life was going pretty much according to our plan. We had been married three years when our daughter, Holly, came into our lives. What a joy she was to us.

Then three years later another baby was on the way, and Jim and I were thrilled. As the weeks and months passed our anticipation grew. Would it be a boy or a girl?

Finally, in the early morning hours of August twenty-fourth, two weeks past her due date, Shelly Anne came into our lives. We now had two little girls. We both rejoiced at what God had done for us.

Then word came from the doctors—our baby girl had multiple problems. We spent New Year's eve in the emergency room where Shelly's life hung in the balance . . . and that was just the beginning. She was unable to sit up, exhibited some mental retardation, had speech problems, and on and on the list went. This was not the road I had planned to take. This was not supposed to be happening . . . but it was.

My life reminded me of the story about a woman who wanted to go on a trip to Italy. She saved her money, learned the language, and planned every aspect of the trip. Finally the day came when she was on the plane headed for Italy. But when the plane landed she heard the flight attendant announce, "Welcome to Holland." She pressed her call button and told the flight attendant that there had to be a mistake. She was supposed to be in Italy. The flight attendant explained, "This plane does not go to Italy." The woman immediately asked when the next plane to Italy would leave, only to have the attendant reply, "I'm sorry, but there are no planes to Italy."

At that moment the woman realized she had two choices. She could spend the rest of her life angry, bitter, and disappointed, or she could embrace Holland and all of it's beauty. Jim and I chose to embrace Shelly and help her become all that was possible for her.

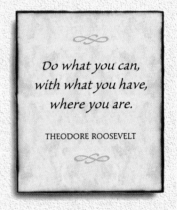

*Do what you can,
with what you have,
where you are.*

THEODORE ROOSEVELT

Where are we now? Shelly has graduated from high school, is driving her own car, and has a job. She's a gold-medal swimmer with the Special Olympics, sings in our church choir, and has been on two mission trips to Honduras and Jamaica. Shelley's life is full of love—a love she shares with everyone she meets. We are all more like Christ because she is part of our lives.

As it turned out, Holland is a beautiful place and, these days, I very rarely think of Italy.

Anne C. Pierson

I'VE TRAVELED LONG I'VE TRAVELED HARD AND STUMBLED MANY TIMES ALONG THE WAY I'VE BRUISED MY KNEES A LOT AND TURNED MY BACK ON GOD AND SEEN HIS MERCY

———————— ❧ ————————

. . . So now I'll walk a different road
I want to see Him there before I even go
I've run ahead and gone too slow I've got to be still now
And wait upon His will now
This time . . . it's gonna be His time

———————— ❧ ————————

. . . I'VE BEEN QUICK TO JUDGE AND SLOW TO LEARN SO MANY TIMES I'VE GOTTEN IN THE WAY I THINK I KNOW SO MUCH I'VE QUESTIONED GOD ENOUGH BUT STILL HE LOVES ME

I'VE TRAVELED LONG I'VE TRAVELED HARD AND STUMBLED MANY TIMES ALONG THE WAY I'VE BRUISED MY KNEES A LOT AND TURNED MY BACK ON GOD AND SEEN HIS MERCY

. . . So now I'll walk a different road

I want to see Him there before I even go

I've run ahead and gone too slow I've got to be still now

And wait upon His will now

This time . . . it's gonna be His time

. . . I'VE BEEN QUICK TO JUDGE AND SLOW TO LEARN SO MANY TIMES I'VE GOTTEN IN THE WAY I THINK I KNOW SO MUCH I'VE QUESTIONED GOD ENOUGH BUT STILL HE LOVES ME

Hurry Up and Guide Me Lord

One week, when my girls were two and three years old, they seemed to be grasping the concept of time in the context of *today, tonight,* and *tomorrow.* Most of their questions that week seemed to revolve around time.

"Mama," Ellie, asked, "when is Mary Peyton coming to my house to play?" Mary was their best friend, and she was going to stay at our house the next day. The girls were already looking forward to playing "mommie" and dress-up with her.

"Honey, I already told you," I answered. "Mary Peyton will be here tomorrow . . . after you eat breakfast."

"No, Mama," Ellie insisted, "I want Mary Peyton to come to my house today!"

I stroked her curly brown hair and explained again, "She'll be here tomorrow, after we wake up and eat our waffles."

Ellie pulled away, pointed her little round finger up at me, and said in her most grown up tone, "No Mama, I want Mary Peyton, *to-now*!"

> *My thoughts are not your thoughts, neither are your ways my ways says the Lord. For as the heavens are higher than the earth, so are my ways higher than your ways and my thoughts than your thoughts.*
>
> ISAIAH 55:8–9

To-now. The word was immediately added to our family vocabulary. I hate to admit it but I've even been using the concept with my heavenly Father. In a journal entry dated January, 1996, I wrote:

Oh God. Why don't you write me a simple little note and send it in the mail? You know, the note that outlines what I'm supposed to be doing down here for You? I'm at the mailbox every day, I'd be sure to receive it. Then I wouldn't have to worry about getting any of Your instructions confused with all the signals that humans (and little humans) are always throwing my way.

A simple little note . . . placed in my simple, little mail box. Oh, and can you send it *to-now?*

Deb Baugher

The Detour

The offer came suddenly. After many years in the music business, I found myself preparing to move cross-country and embark on a new adventure as personal assistant to a rock-and-roll legend.

I had paid my dues to get this job and was eagerly anticipating a new life with all the perks—condo, salary, prestige. In just four months my new journey would begin.

With four months to "burn," I found a short-term job recruiting students for a Christian college. I enjoyed the work and was thankful for the provision, but kept in mind that this was just a detour. It would never appear on a resume, and I was looking forward to getting back on the road again.

But driving between appointments one day I listened to a national broadcast about Angel Tree—a division of Prison Fellowship that provides Christmas presents for prisoners' children. That same day, as I listened to the music of a prominent Christian artist, a seed was planted.

Within days I heard myself pitching a tour concept to a senior executive at ministry headquarters and proposing myself as the best candidate for the job. Meanwhile, the job of a lifetime waited in Sun Valley.

In his heart a man plans his course, but the Lord determines his steps.

PROVERBS 16:9

As you can probably guess, I never made it to Idaho. I went into prison and began working to bring Christ to the inmates. Five years later I still work with musicians, but backstage passes and press conferences aren't part of my life. I design evangelism campaigns to reach eighty percent of prisoners who don't attend religious services. To do this we take musicians, comedians, and sports figures into the prisons.

There are no tour buses, no five-star hotels, and no backstage catering. It's the hardest job I've ever had—but also the most gratifying. It was just a four-month detour, but God used it to change my life. A wise man once told me to follow the road as far as I could see and God would meet me there. My heart is full of thanks for the miles down the road that we can't see and everything God has waiting there . . . even the detours.

Robyn Anderson

A saint is not one who never falls;
it is one who gets up and goes
on every time he falls.

Anonymous

Held Close to God's Heart

Their youthful smoothness is diffused by a rougher texture, their porcelain complexion splashed with amber. They hold the power to silence and the tenderness to calm. They are my mother's hands.

Her hands are not perfect, but they are beautiful for they represent a heart of charity, a heart of diligence, even a heart of peace. Now, I see the resemblance. They are my hands, too, and oh, how I hope these hands reflect not just the heart of my mother but, ultimately, the hands and heart of God!

Touching the eyes of the blind, the Messiah announced, "According to your faith you are healed." So may I touch the spiritually blind and help lead them to faith.

Jesus placed His hands upon the children and blessed them. In patience and joy, in peace and guidance, may my hands demonstrate the eternal goodness of Christ to my precious children.

Like a gentle shepherd, Christ "gathers the lambs in His arms and carries them close to His heart." May I see each person as one of Jesus' lambs, that my arms might hold the hurting, embrace the searching, and greet the unwelcome.

> ∞
>
> We are God's workmanship, created in Christ Jesus to do good works which God prepared in advance for us to do.
>
> EPHESIANS 2:10
>
> ∞

Christ's hands carry the solace to heal a broken heart and the comfort to calm a troubled spirit. How I pray that even in my human, faltering way, my hands would hold His goodness, His mercy, His compassion. And when my hands grow wrinkled with age, I will view each line as a mark of wisdom, each blemish as a reminder of work done throughout the years for God's glory—just as my mother's hands did.

Tamara L. Tilley

A note from Kathy Troccoli:

You will often hear me say to my audiences that our stories are the same.

Different pages, different chapters, different seasons—but our struggles, our fears, our dark days and our days of glory are the same—as we battle with our humanity to abandon ourselves to an extraordinary God. We can all become embittered or empowered. Shake our fists at heaven or shake our fists at hell. Run in circles or walk in His shadow. Be consumed by our passions or live passionately for Him.

God's Message to Me

I stood looking at the clumps of dust collected behind our television set without the slightest motivation to vacuum it.

What difference would it make? I asked myself.
After all, we are no more than specks of dust ourselves, like insignificant ants, seen from an airplane, scurrying around in futility.

It had been ten years since I'd graduated from college, and I still carried with me the remnants of my philosophy, mythology, and psychology courses. I doubted God existed. When I tried to pray, my prayers seem to dissipate. After all, why pray to the most fabricated fairy tale of all time? Weren't Adam and Eve just another myth, much like the origin myths of ancient pagan societies? How could I believe the Bible was true and that God truly did exist?

Yet I simply had to know if God was real, so I asked Him to break through my doubts and reveal Himself to me. Although skeptical, I started to read the Bible, gradually exposing myself to its truths. As I read, I learned about the attributes of God: He is our heavenly Father, He is faithful, and He is our protector.

I have come that they may have life and have it to the full.

JOHN 10:10

One day, still pondering the reality of God, I went outside to check on my daughters who were playing in the backyard. As I walked along the deck, I heard the loud call of a bird and looked up to see a brilliant red cardinal perched on a branch. Immediately, I felt the bird had called to me. I didn't understand it, but I knew it was significant—and I knew it had to do with God.

Later that afternoon while I was leafing through the mail, I noticed an advertisement for a beautiful porcelain statue of a cardinal perched on a branch. Somehow I knew God wanted me to pay close attention to this. As I read the material my jaw

dropped in excitement and awe. The pamphlet listed the attributes of the male bird: he's a faithful mate, a loving father, and a fierce defender of his family.

I started to cry. I knew beyond a shadow of doubt this was God's message to me. The Creator of the universe was communicating with me. He loved me and wanted me to know that He was real. I was not an insignificant ant. I was God's precious child—the apple of His eye.

I am blessed to know God, and now, whatever I do, even dusting behind the television set, I do it all for Him.

Jennifer Esposito

God Walks the Road with Me

When I was a young Christian I never wanted to hear about sickness, sorrow, or death. Those things didn't happen to Christians. But now, having lived through sorrow, I have learned to accept it as one of God's special graces.

When my lovely mother died not long ago, I suffered such deep sadness. Even after she was gone I could still hear her voice. The smell of her clothes left me weeping.

Yet out of my despair I realized new things about heaven. I had prayed and believed that Mother would survive liver cancer, but God wanted her Home. My mother was a vibrant woman who believed in God. I knew without doubt that she was in heaven. Where else could she be? Certainly not in some ethereal, far-off place. Suddenly, heaven became almost tangible. It was indeed a real place. It was my mother's new residence, and the place where I, too, would live one day.

> I am convinced that life is ten percent what happens to me and ninety percent how I react to it.
>
> CHARLES R. SWINDOLL

Grief gave me a deeper longing for eternity and a more intimate relationship with God. There is a strange beauty in the midst of sorrow. I found God there in a way I had never experienced Him before. The sadness of life took me down a different road. But the Sovereign God walked down that road with me, and by His grace the blessings of sorrow taught me to keep my eyes on heaven.

Elissa Musumeci

God Designed This Road for Me

Upon graduating from college, I began climbing the corporate ladder in an international costume jewelry company. At age twenty-nine, I was one step away from the highest position in the company.

I was responsible for thirty-seven employees—most of whom were old enough to be my father—and one training director. My salary increased to six figures. My husband and I were living the proverbial good life . . . but something was missing.

Gradually, my desire to scale the next hurdle diminished, and I found myself yearning for something—rather someone—I had never thought about: a baby. These new feelings were fleeting but real. They would peak when a co-worker became pregnant or a friend gave birth. It wasn't long before the desire for motherhood became overwhelming.

It took about three years for me to acknowledge God's plan. During that time I suffered from mental fatigue and from something much, much worse—the anguish of two miscarriages and the despair of infertility. After enduring countless tests and fertility drugs, I began to believe I would never have a child. I prayed more and slept less.

When my best friend became pregnant, I was ecstatic for her but heartbroken for my own empty arms. I shook my fist at heaven and cried, "Haven't you heard my prayers, God?" I sat and wept. Suddenly, a still small voice spoke to my heart the word *Ruth*. Immediately, my spirit understood. I ran to my Bible and the verse I was drawn to took my breath away: "And now, my daughter, don't be afraid. I will do for you all you ask. All my fellow townsmen know that you are a woman of noble character" (Ruth 3:11).

God had heard my prayer! Someday I would be a mother! My spirit rejoiced.

> Behold, I am the Lord, the God of all flesh; is anything too hard for me?
>
> JEREMIAH 32:27

As my husband and I used the promises from God's Word to silence the doubts of doctors and loved ones, our faith grew strong. With a small band of believers, we prayed fervently for the day when we would be blessed with a little boy. I began to anticipate the day I would hold a baby in my arms.

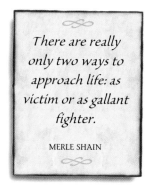

There are really only two ways to approach life: as victim or as gallant fighter.

MERLE SHAIN

What joy filled our hearts a year and a half later when our "trinity baby," Nicholas Robert Gardner, came into the world, a fulfillment of God's promise. Less than three years later our daughter was born, and right now we are expecting our third child.

The road I chose for myself almost ten years ago is unrecognizable to me now. The road God has designed for me to walk is more challenging than anything I encountered in the business world—and much more fulfilling. I'm so thankful He chose me to be His daughter and allowed me to be a mother.

Donna Gardner

Our Heavenly Father
Never Leaves Us

My heart sank as I reached the top of the chair lift. Written ominously on one of those "Contact Ski Patrol" message boards was my last name. It couldn't be good. It wasn't.

My mentor, my biggest fan—my dad—had just died. He had suffered a massive heart attack in the elevator between the second and third floors of the company he founded. How could it be? We had just skied together the week before. Suddenly, he was no longer there to share his wise advice or to give cherished encouragement.

Dad was a bold man. He never shied away from challenging conventional wisdom or seizing an opportunity—whether in business or in God's work. I inherited some of that tendency, but soon after his death I realized my boldness didn't carry into every area of my life, particularly in sharing my faith with others.

> *Nothing is so strong as gentleness, nothing so gentle as real strength.*
>
> ST. FRANCIS DE SALES

I was comfortable in the knowledge of my Heavenly Father. Confident of the eternal life I've been promised through Jesus Christ. But share my assurance of salvation with others? The thought occasionally crossed my mind but was always met with reluctance. It's scary to share those things. It's personal. It's risky. I might not explain things just right, or I might offend someone.

But with the death of my earthly father came a deeper realization of my Heavenly Father's constancy and faithfulness.

He is *always* there, and He longs for us to rest in His arms. How can I *not* share that truth with those who do not know His faithfulness? Who don't know the joy of a relationship with an Eternal Father?

God, our Father, never leaves us. He loves us in spite of ourselves, regardless how many times we mess things up. I can't help but share those truths more boldly today.

Betsy DeVos

DON'T WANT TO LIVE WITHOUT THE PEACE THAT COMES TO ME
WHEN I AM BY HIS SIDE I'VE KNOWN THE FREEDOM THERE
CAN'T FIND IT ANYWHERE BUT IN CHRIST JESUS

——————— ∽ ———————

. . . So now I'll walk a different road
I want to see Him there before I even go
I've run ahead and gone too slow I've got to be still now
And wait upon His will now
This time . . . it's gonna be His time

——————— ∽ ———————

. . . I BELIEVE HE'S GOT A PLAN EVERYTHING IN HIS TIME I
MAY NOT ALWAYS UNDERSTAND EVERYTHING IN HIS TIME
EVERYTHING IN HIS TIME

DON'T WANT TO LIVE WITHOUT THE PEACE THAT COMES TO ME

WHEN I AM BY HIS SIDE I'VE KNOWN THE FREEDOM THERE

CAN'T FIND IT ANYWHERE BUT IN CHRIST JESUS

. . . So now I'll walk a different road

I want to see Him there before I ever go

I've run ahead and gone too slow I've got to be still now

And wait upon His will now

This time . . . it's gonna be His time

. . . I BELIEVE HE'S GOT A PLAN EVERYTHING IN HIS TIME I

MAY NOT ALWAYS UNDERSTAND EVERYTHING IN HIS TIME

EVERYTHING IN HIS TIME

A note from Kathy Troccoli:

As an emotional and fragile woman who has faced many valleys and "dark nights of the soul," I can speak to you sincerely and confidently about the unwavering love and mercy of Jesus Christ.

I am single yet comforted by the ultimate bridegroom.

I was orphaned by having two young parents taken from this earth but have been adopted by the Father of the Fatherless.

I have struggled with weight issues and yet continue to hear Him affirm my femininity with words of beauty as He escorts me through this life.

I can worry about finances, and He'll reassure me that His eye is on the sparrow.

When I'm prideful He humbly embraces me.

My self-esteem hits all-time lows, and He'll whisper my worth through the cross.

I've forsaken Him. He's forgiven me.

I'll get hit with waves of anxiety and doubt, and He'll allow me to ride above them to shores of truth and safety as I learn to put my trust in Him.

My Different Road

As often happens, we take the roundabout way, into dark alleys, down the left fork of the road, through the thickets of the woods until we find the right road, the high road. Let me tell you when this happened to me.

I was forty-two, living in New York, and successfully running my own company. But I felt it was time to take an honest look at my life and my relationship with God. Call it a mid-life assessment, if you will. So I began to study the book *Experiencing God* with the women in my church and prayed for a change in my life.

Then my sister called to say that Mom was in the hospital with pneumonia. I was on the next plane to Alabama.

Mom is the strongest woman I've ever known. She served in the Air Force during World War II, had three children and more than her share of miscarriages, taught school through all of my growing-up years, led scouts, taught Sunday school, and gave piano lessons. She instilled in my brother and sister and me a spirit of adventure, a love for learning, and an unshakeable faith. She buried my dad, buried my thirty-four-year old brother, and drove herself to the hospital the day she was admitted for pneumonia. She's no weakling.

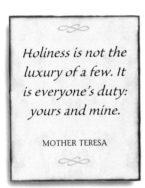

Holiness is not the luxury of a few. It is everyone's duty: yours and mine.

MOTHER TERESA

So when the doctor informed us she had congestive heart failure, I thought, "She's resilient, she'll make it through this." For the next few days I became her cheerleader and spiritual encourager, but her condition didn't improve. She had a seizure and was placed in ICU. She lost complete control of all of her muscles. She couldn't walk, think straight, eat, or take care of herself. My strong, independent mother became an invalid.

While I called my office every day and returned phone calls, for the most part I was totally detached from my own circumstances to serve Mom and love her back to health. That was when I learned the real reason I was in Alabama.

One morning while I was getting ready to leave for the hospital, I heard God whisper, *"This isn't about your mom, Cindy. It's about you."* I was perplexed but listened further. *"Your mother being hospitalized is a catalyst for My will to be fulfilled in your life. I want you to know Me in a new way, so you will love others more deeply, more fully."* In that moment I began to seek forgiveness for my lack of faith, my fear and anxiety over my future. I felt comforted by God's presence, and my spirit was renewed.

In the days ahead, I began to look at Mom in a different light, to love her with a new and sincere devotion. I noticed the nurses and doctors with more detail and softened my approach to be more loving toward them. Mom's three-month stay in the hospital was my God-given sabbatical.

After another three weeks of therapy, Mom returned with me to New York. If anyone had told me I would love having Mom with me for three months in a cramped one-bedroom apartment, I would have said, "Well, I'll do it, but it won't be easy." Yet it turned out to be one of the greatest experiences of my life. I had Mom back from a debilitating illness and now loved her in a miraculous way—unconditionally, without judgment. When she sang a hymn or read the paper out loud while I was doing something, instead of trying to ignore her, I stopped what I was doing to give her my full attention. I found new life in sharing this very special woman with my friends. They loved to visit her and would ask her to sing one of the great radio hits from the thirties and forties.

Eventually, Mom totally regained her health and was able to return to Alabama. She visits me twice a year now, for two months at a time, and these are some of the most rewarding days of my life. God knew I needed to love my mother with a deep, unconditional love before I could walk closer to Him. This experience was a refiner's fire, directing me down a different road—a road that would help me become more like Christ.

Cindy Dupree

God Restores Our Joy

I looked at the faces of the women sitting in front of me and remembered the miracle that had brought me here.

These women and I were gathered on a mountain in Tennessee for a three-day retreat from the craziness of our lives. But to me it was more than a three-day retreat. Only a year before, in this same place, I had come to another retreat called Joy Springs, but I had come with anything but joy. I was going through the most hopeless and desperate time of my life.

For two years prior to that I had been in a place of utter brokenness. Difficult circumstances had led me to an empass of my faith. My natural inclination was to run away from that retreat, to avoid facing the "dark night" of my soul.

Yet somehow I knew that if I stayed and made the spiritual journey, my life would never be the same. I also knew that God would be more real to me than He had ever been before. Both of these things happened . . . and it all began right on the mountain.

During that retreat, nestled away in the beauty of the mountains, God supernaturally restored my joy. One morning, as we began to sing and worship, I heard a man's faint laughter. It reminded me of the name of the retreat—Joy Springs! I felt God whisper to my heart, *"I have brought you here to restore your joy."* I raised my hands to thank Him, and in that moment great joy flooded my soul.

> *Come to me, all you who are weary and burdened, and I will give you rest.*
>
> MATTHEW 11:28

Now, a year later, I was returning to that same mountain a different person. Instead of coming to receive, I had been sent to give. For three days I was going to talk and share the reality of God and His desire to work in our lives and our marriages.

A year ago God had allowed me to come to my Mt. Moriah, and when I walked up the mountain He offered a ram in the thicket. Like Abraham, I have never been the same. If we learn anything in this journey of life, we need to remember not to run from the walk up the mountain because our joy and deliverance waits just ahead. God longs to reveal Himself as our Deliverer, the One who will change our lives forever.

Denise G. Hildreth

God's Plan for the Mountains and the Valleys

Imagine if a friend told you she could load a software program onto your computer that would revolutionize your life.

It would have a positive effect on everyone and everything you touch. It would handle so many of life's problems that you'd be free to be the wife, mother, friend, or daughter that you long to be. It would give you rest and peace. But in order for the program to work you would have to change the way you input information. In fact, in order to load it into your computer you would have to delete all existing programs. Even the most basic every day tasks that you perform so comfortably would have to be changed.

Philippians 4:6-7, "be anxious for nothing," is that "program" for me. It requires that I abandon comfortable patterns of behavior, that I change how I think and how I respond to difficulty and trials. It encourages me to choose a new way that promises peace beyond human understanding.

I made this discovery a year ago when I lost a steady source of income that had carried me through times when work as a musician was sparse. The loss of this security was traumatic, especially when it happened just a month before I was scheduled to go on a mission trip to Europe. I had already raised funds to cover the trip, but this meant I'd be coming home without a cent and with no income in sight. My natural inclination was to become fearful and anxious. Trusting God for finances had always been a weakness for me.

But He challenged me to lay my fears at the foot of the cross and humbly seek Him for direction. I had to *choose* not to worry. The words I spoke had to change. Instead of rehearsing my problems in conversation with friends, I began to affirm God's faithfulness. When worry flooded my mind I chose to believe God had a plan. I thanked Him for what He was doing that I couldn't see. I prayed specifically for His wisdom and direction.

I prayed some bold prayers during that time. I asked God to make me a woman of radical faith. Events began to unfold that were unquestionably divine. My mission trip would be over at the end of August, but before we left I was invited to work with a touring musical group, starting in September. Right on time! Instrument endorsements started coming my way. Every time I was obedient to give money God told me to give, He returned it to me in some of the most unexpected ways, and with a bonus.

As I look back over my mountain top and valley experiences, I marvel at the faithfulness of God in both places. Even when I was not pursuing Him, He never stopped giving me good things. What I have chosen for my "new program" or "different road" are these biblical principles:

- Don't worry about anything.
- Take everything to God in prayer and leave it there.
- Maintain a thankful heart.

There are certain to be storms ahead, but I want to walk through them with confidence in God, knowing the peace that only He can give.

Valerie Clemente

I Know Who I Am in Christ

One morning in the upstairs hallway I overheard Grandmother say to Mom "Oh my God! I pray Dorothy doesn't die young like your sister did."

I was only ten years old at the time, but I can still remember the terrible fear that gripped me. That night I cried myself to sleep—a dreadful seed of fear had been planted in my heart.

Whenever I got sick my grandmother's words rang loud in my ears and I wondered, *"Is this when I'm going to die?"* It didn't help that death was all around me. For as long as I can remember my mom was plagued with heart disease and, later, diabetes. Going to the hospital to visit her was as natural as going to Grandma's for Sunday dinner. I was always excited when Dad would tell me Mom was coming home. But after she was home for a few days, anxiety and fear would overcome me. At night I would tiptoe into her room and lean over her as she slept to see if she was still breathing.

Nineteen years later Mom died. She was fifty-six, and I, at the young age of twenty-nine, wondered how long *I* had to live.

A year later I rededicated my life to Christ. However, the seed of fear, planted long ago, was even greater now. It was a roaring lion in my life. Soon I began to date a godly young man who eventually became my husband. In obedience to God, he challenged me to deal with my fear. Whenever I felt sick and gave in to my fear of death, my husband would direct me to the Word of God. Slowly I was released from the chains that held me captive for years.

> *The key question in life is not "How strong am I?" but rather "How strong is God?"*
>
> MAX LUCADO

Yet it wasn't long before my faith was put to the test. In a routine checkup, the doctor found a tumor on my ovaries. I knew that if I gave in to my fear it would destroy me, so I embraced the Word of God like never before. I underwent surgery, and the doctors discovered endometriosis, which led to further surgery. The doctor found a tumor in my uterus that could not be removed, yet when I went for a follow-up exam six months later the tumor was gone!

I stand in awe of what God has done in my life. He has purified my heart and strengthened my faith. Fear no longer rules me, for I know who I am in Christ.

Dorothy Ophals

The Sometimes Long and Winding Road

Abandonment. What a sad and lonely word. It's a word I've lived with since I was fourteen.

Just after my birthday that year I had to cope with the horrific news that my mom was dying of pancreatic cancer. After Mom died, my sister and her family moved away, and my brother joined the Army, leaving me to cope with the pain on my own. Then for no reason that made sense to me, my dog was put to sleep. I was terribly sad and lonely. I felt totally abandoned.

Why me, God?

The next year I met the boy of my dreams. Courtship and marriage followed, and we enjoyed sixteen years of marriage. Filled with what I thought was pure bliss and joy. I had someone to love me, take care of me, and want me forever.

Suddenly, overnight, my "perfect" life was gone. My husband decided after all those years of marriage to tell me, "This isn't working." I was enveloped in disbelief, heartache, and abandonment. I wondered why God was doing this to me again.

Why me God? Not again.

It has taken many years, but now I see that God has a perfect plan for my life. My mom went to be with Him in 1964, and through her illness He made me a stronger, yet more caring, person. He filled a void of loneliness in my life with my husband, and gave me happiness, strength, and understanding. Even when I found myself alone again after more than twenty years of marriage, God guided me and gave me wisdom to live on my own.

The Lord is close to the brokenhearted and saves those who are crushed in spirit.

PSALM 34:18

Out of that aloneness, I have bonded with my family, and they have become some of my dearest friends. I am so thankful that God helped me to become an independent woman, proud of my life and my accomplishments. He has given me wonderful and cherished friends, who have given me amazing support.

All of our roads are long and winding, with obstacles in the way. I've hit a number of them, sometimes making the right decisions and sometimes making the wrong ones. But through it all, God's hand is at work. He forgives me and helps me to pick myself up, brush myself off, and continue down the road.

Linda M. Taddei

Holding on with Faith

I watched my mother fight with all her efforts to live longer than the doctors predicted. Her youngest child was to be married in just a few short weeks, and she was going to see that day through.

With a display of the most amazing fortitude, Mom lived till the day after the wedding. Although she was in a coma for three days prior to the wedding, on that day with a new bride and groom, all her children and grandchildren in her hospital room, her tired eyes opened to acknowledge that she *had* made it to the wedding. Tears and joy choked inside my throat. I felt both pain at her condition and yet pride in the strength of her spirit.

I remember sitting in the hospital room and considering my own death. I wondered how I would die. Would my life exude a wondrous peace of God that told all around me of a solid faith in Him? I guess sitting there watching the end of a life, I focused hard on my nice, clean, simple evangelical beliefs. If my life were to end right then, would I be in eternity with God? Even though shaken by Satan's devastating vacuum of death, I knew then and there that I would indeed be in heaven in the very presence of God Almighty.

I do not know that I will ever be without the ache of missing Mom. But the experience of death has caused me to hold white-knuckled to the very hem of the robe of my Savior, and know that I am His.

Georgina A. Godfrey

Walking Down a Different Road

I took a vow never to marry. It was a solemn promise, made to myself, that I couldn't and wouldn't involve myself in the institution of marriage.

I believed that the job of *wife* and *mother* was clearly a vocation I was unprepared and unsuited for. Mothers were soft, patient, and understanding; they enjoyed being around children. I was independent—a busy go-getter. From early baby-sitting days, I knew I was not cut out for childcare. I was twenty-seven, successful in a top sales position, and enjoying my own home, expensive sports car, and all the essential non-essentials that told me who I was. I had no room for marriage.

About this time, I broke off yet another relationship with a godly man—the last in a long line that always ended at the point of commitment. The only difference this time was that I finally felt curious as to *why*. What I did know was that my resistance to marriage was solemn and strong. It would take divine intervention to untangle me.

As I look back now, I can see that God used the three things He always uses to set us free from our foolishness: His Word, His people, and His Spirit. I was studying for my masters degree in counseling and began to look at the Genesis account of creation. I was intrigued with the idea that God created some uniquely male and others uniquely female. I began to wonder what it meant to live out my femininity according to His design. If I had been created to receive a man, what was blocking my way?

> *In the depth of winter, I finally learned that within me there lay an invincible summer.*
>
> ALBERT CAMUS

There were many things to consider, but what became obvious was that I had made a stubborn commitment to stay isolated and alone. I asked God to forgive me and to change this attitude. God also began to dismantle my vow through the example of other believers around me. I saw how they honored their marriage vows. They modeled bold love and an unwavering commitment to see God's work played out not only in their own lives but in the life of their marriage partner as well. This intrigued me and unnerved me. My heart began to soften and, gradually, I began to dream . . . to hope . . . to desire all that God intended for me—including marriage, if that was His will.

As clearly as I remember taking my vow, I remember breaking it. I saw him from a distance and watched him walk across a crowded room at a conference. A wave of joy swept across my heart because I knew that if this man would pursue me, I was ready to receive and to give, ready to leave behind the vow that had kept me safe and alone.

It is five years later now. I am happily married to that very man and have three delightful sons. I have made a promise to involve myself totally in the work of being a *wife* and *mother*. And who would have guessed . . . I am soft and patient and love to be around children!

Allyson R. Baker

The Road to the Richest Part of Life

This week marks the thirtieth anniversary of an event that changed my life. It marked a turning point where my life took a different road.

As a high school freshman, I was involved in a basketball game that had taken the student body and community fans some ninety miles away from our small hometown. Suddenly, the superintendent's wife came up to me and asked me to step outside for a moment. She said that on his way to the game, my older brother had been involved in a head-on collision. I remember her saying that the other two passengers in the car were both dead—she didn't know if my brother was alive or not.

For the next several hours, as they drove me to the hospital, I cried and prayed—bargaining with God for my brother's life. It seemed like an eternity until we reached the hospital and found out that he had survived the accident and would recover. Later that night I stood outside his hospital room while my parents told him that his two friends hadn't survived the crash. I'll never forget that agonizing moment and how despairingly he cried.

My brother was never quite the same after that tragedy. The following year we pulled up stakes and moved to Oklahoma City. This proved to be the best for my brother as well as our whole family. A bigger city provided greater spiritual opportunities and advantages we would never have had in a small town.

> *Perseverance is not a long race; it is many short races one after another.*
>
> WALTER ELLIOT

Through the years I've reached out to my older brother and he to me. I find him changed, yet full of a depth that understands the fragility of life and appreciates time spent with friends and family. Great tragedies reshape our lives, leading us down a new and different road, and often it's the difficulties along the way that eventually lead us to the sweetest, richest parts of life.

Pamela Muse

No More Wandering for Me

The guest speaker told our congregation that Moses spent the first forty years of his life thinking he was somebody . . . the next forty realizing he was nobody . . . and the forty after that discovering what God could accomplish through a humble nobody.

This analysis was of great interest to me, especially in light of the fact that I have embarked upon "the second forty."

Life as I knew it came to a startling halt when my husband accepted a position with an international ministry based in Washington D.C. I had spent my entire life within a twenty-five-mile radius, enjoying deep roots, a long history, and a wide comfort zone. Moving away from all this was the beginning of a humbling process, a pruning season in my life.

Nothing was familiar. There were no points of reference, warm fuzzies, or meaningful memories. I found it difficult to gain entry to hearts and homes. I had "performed" well in the past, and I resolved to do so again. I decided the solution was to make meaningful contributions to the school, the church, and the community. Surely, my gifts would be appreciated and welcomed. Surely the school board, the PTA, and the women's ministry team would see that I had leadership skills and a wealth of experience. They would be glad for what I could contribute.

But for the first time in my life, I didn't find acceptance and unconditional love. Suddenly, my motives were questioned and my strengths looked upon as weaknesses. I felt like I was in a dry, forsaken desert . . . and oh, so thirsty. *God, how could you bring me out here to die?*

His response came in bits and pieces, sometimes with a gentle brush stroke and other times with a fierce sword. I was forced to come to terms with some difficult truths. I had been smug and arrogant about avoiding deadly sins and had no patience for those who lacked the strength and discipline to do the same. Compassion, mercy, and humility were *not* my trademarks. I was guilty of the most deadly sin: pride.

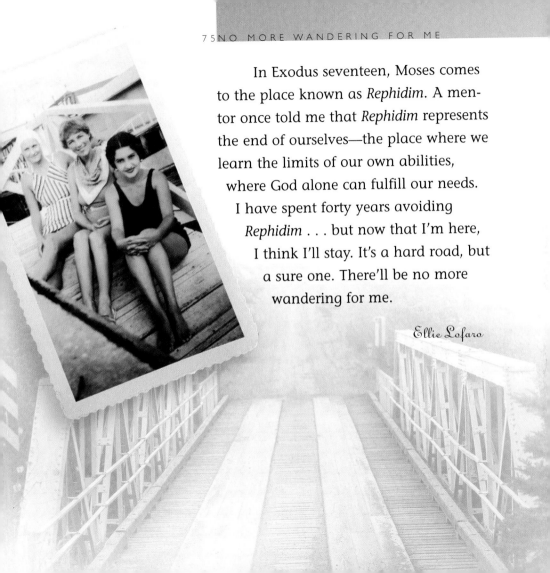

In Exodus seventeen, Moses comes to the place known as *Rephidim*. A mentor once told me that *Rephidim* represents the end of ourselves—the place where we learn the limits of our own abilities, where God alone can fulfill our needs. I have spent forty years avoiding *Rephidim* . . . but now that I'm here, I think I'll stay. It's a hard road, but a sure one. There'll be no more wandering for me.

Ellie Lofaro

Finding God in the Little Things

I first learned about trust from my dad. Who wouldn't trust this big, kind, gentle man?

The man who carefully provided for our family and played with us. The man who held my little body close at the ocean and said, "You are safe in my arms." The man who prayed to God when I was hurt or sick or fearful.

I was a young adult when we learned that Dad had Alzheimer's disease. I went before God and prayed . . . and begged . . . and pleaded . . . and bargained for my father's health and mind to return. I waited and hoped for many years. But slowly, I became angry and began to doubt God. How could the God my dad loved and served not heal him?

Doubt and anger grew deeper and darker. I felt like I was falling—falling into pain and depression. I smiled and was strong on the outside, but inside I was screaming and dying. With my back turned from God, I couldn't shake the fear and loneliness; I was frightened of the person I was becoming.

> *Although the world is very full of suffering, it is also full of overcoming of it.*
>
> HELEN KELLER

Yet deep inside my heart somewhere I desperately wanted to trust God, to rest in Him… and eventually I did. Ever so slowly my heart began to see light, to feel God again. Not through lightening from the sky but through little things. I saw God in my mother's life. She had lost her husband, yet she continued to serve God with joy. I saw Him in the love of the children I was teaching, and in the patience of a friend.

God spoke gently to me from His Word, and I began to hope again. My relationship with Him became real. Like the lost sheep in Luke 15, God gently gathered me into His arms and carried me close. The valley that was low became raised; the rough ground became level (Isaiah 40:4, 11).

Allison M. H. Trifoli

Sophie and
her flowers

... are ...
... your new ...
... father has ...
... times about my ...
... goods, ...
... answer ...
... make to this ...
... sold ...
... that ...
... and ...
... packed ready ...
... my, Write ...
... Read...

Self-Worth

It's hard to focus in on other people and what you can do for them when you don't feel worthy of love yourself. When you feel that you could not possibly have anything to offer to anyone else.

I grew up in a home of ultimate control. My thoughts and feelings could not be my own but had to coincide with those of my parents. I never learned how to be "me," apart from them. I found myself, a thirty-three year old woman, married and the mother of two children, yet still feeling like a child. I had confidence in all the "stuff" on the outside, because the package wasn't too shabby, but felt empty and childlike on the inside. I had an emptiness within. I was searching for something that my soul needed, but I didn't know what it was.

Just like He had throughout my life, God gently led me where I needed to be. I began to see a Christian counselor, who encouraged me to read a book that helped change my life. I learned that because we are created in God's image we have stewardship over our time, talents, feelings, and values. Because I had never developed a sense of "mine," I had no sense of responsibility to develop and nurture these resources. I didn't think "me" was worth anything. But if I didn't believe I was worth anything, how could I give of myself to anyone else? How could I give to God?

Finally, after two years of struggle, with God on one side and a kind and understanding husband on the other, it happened. I was able to see that I *do* matter, that I have gifts to offer. I know now that I am worthy to be loved and to love others—but most of all to be loved by God! Yes, even He can love me!

Anne Marie Spiliotis

Stronger for the Journey

At age fifteen, Vicky had everything to live for. Bright, energetic, and enthusiastic, she had no way of knowing that her life was about to change drastically. And I had no way of knowing how profoundly that would affect mine.

Without warning, a numbness and pain in her cheek was diagnosed as a rare cancer that had already spread. Thus began a never-ending series of radiation, chemotherapy, and experimental medication that brought a seesaw of hope and despair. There were critical times when her life hung in the balance and moments of joy when remission and miracles intermingled.

It was shortly after her diagnosis that a friend first invited me to come and pray for healing with Vicky. I was eager to share the truths of Christ with this young woman whose name meant *victory!* Seeing her in those early days was a joy. Her bright red hair, blue eyes, and winning smile always welcomed us. We'd talk about the day, admire some new craft she had made, and share the gospel.

By the end of January, Vicky took a turn for the worst. One evening I called to check on her condition and to confirm my visit for the following day. To my surprise, her father answered the telephone. Her parents had been divorced prior to Vicky's illness and their relationship was strained. The urgency in his voice let me know that tomorrow might be too late.

Within minutes I arrived to find Vicky conscious but in a very weakened state. Once again my tears flowed freely as I told her that she was my hero. I could hear her laugh beneath her labored breathing. I was privileged to witness God's love for Vicky in a powerful way. There, praying beside her bed was her mother, her father, and her brother. Because of the strain that divorce and separation had brought, this was a moment only God could have orchestrated. Vicky's prayer for her family had always been that there would be peace.

Here around her deathbed, God had allowed her to see His hand in that situation.

The peace of God so filled the room that I didn't want to leave, but the time had come to say good-bye. Still hoping for a miracle I promised I would be back the following day. "I'll see you again Vicky," I said as I kissed her parched face. "Thank you for everything" she whispered.

Early the next morning God took Vicky home. Her struggles were over. Her battle was won. Her healing was complete. As I thought back to our weekly visits, I remembered particularly our times of prayer, when it seemed like God's peace filled her very being and radiated from her face. I always left her home feeling as if I had been healed . . . healed of my self-centeredness and complaining. Yes, I will always be thankful for Vicky. She enriched my life and strengthened my journey with Christ beyond measure.

Breeda W. Connolly

The Big C

"Michele, it's cancer." With those three simple words I began a journey down the road of the big C: cancer.

As a pastor's wife with a radio program, I had always encouraged my audience to trust God in every circumstance of life, not walking in fear but in "love, power, and a sound mind." Now it was my turn.

When I walked into the hospital that afternoon, I was unaware of the biopsy results. I didn't realize that the evil finger of cancer had violated my body, that there was an invasive malignant tumor in my left breast. But God had assured me that my life was in His hands, and I was determined to trust Him no matter what report I received.

Yet when I heard those three words a shock wave went through my body. How would I tell my three children and two grandchildren that Nana was sick but they need not be afraid? My husband and I walked down the hallway with the words cancer, surgery, and treatment staring us in the face. I remember thinking, *"I don't have time for this! Will I lose my breast? Or my hair? Will I see my new granddaughter?"* We had walked through hard places before, but this was unexpected.

Still there were glimpses of God's mercy even in that dark valley. When I asked God if I would be healed instantly or through the process, He spoke Psalm 23:4 to my heart. "Even though I walk through the darkest valley, I will not fear for you are close beside me." I was walking one of the most difficult roads of my life, but I knew God would lead every step of the way.

> *Your circumstances have absolutely nothing to do with God's ability to perform His word.*
>
> OSWALD CHAMBERS

The day of surgery arrived. I had chosen the lumpectomy followed by chemotherapy and radiation treatments. Before entering the operating room I had one request: I wanted to hear my favorite song, "My Life Is in Your Hands."

After the surgery I woke up to the news that the tumor had literally popped out! And the recovery room nurse gave me a word she had received from the Lord: "blessed assurance"—my favorite hymn! I remember gasping with joy underneath the oxygen mask. Yes, I knew with a blessed assurance that my life truly was in God's hands.

Michele K. O'Dell

You never really lose until you quit trying.

Mike Ditka